The Scheme of Driftless Shifter

by Carolyn Lane

Baker's Plays
7611 Sunset Blvd.
Los Angeles, CA 90042
bakersplays.com

NOTICE

This book is offered for sale at the price quoted only on the understanding that, if any additional copies of the whole or any part are necessary for its production, such additional copies will be purchased. The attention of all purchasers is directed to the following: this work is fully protected under the copyright laws of the United States of America, the British Commonwealth, including Canada, and all other countries of the Copyright Union. Violations of the Copyright Law are punishable by fine or imprisonment, or both. The copying or duplication of this work or any part of this work, by hand or by any process, is an infringement of the copyright and will be vigorously prosecuted.

This play may not be produced by amateurs or professionals for public or private performance without first submitting application for performing rights. Royalties are due on all performances whether for charity or gain, or whether admission is charged or not. Since performance of this play without the payment of the royalty fee renders anybody participating liable to severe penalties imposed by the law, anybody acting in this play should be sure, before doing so, that the royalty fee has been paid. Professional rights, reading rights, radio broadcasting, television and all mechanical rights, etc. are strictly reserved. Application for performing rights should be made directly to BAKER'S PLAYS.

No one shall commit or authorize any act or omission by which the copyright of, or the right to copyright, this play may be impaired. No one shall make any changes in this play for the purpose of production.

Publication of this play does not imply availability for performance. Both amateurs and professionals considering a production are strongly advised in their own interest to apply to Baker's Plays for written permission before starting rehearsals, advertising, or booking a theatre.

Whenever the play is produced, the author's name must be carried in all publicity, advertising and programs. Also, the following notice must appear on all printed programs, "Produced by special arrangement with Baker's Plays."

Licensing fees for *THE SCHEME OF THE DRIFTLESS SHIFTER* is based on a per performance rate and payable one week in advance of the production.

Please consult the Baker's Plays website at www.bakersplays.com or our current print catalogue for up to date licensing fee information.

THE SCHEME OF THE DRIFTLESS SHIFTER
ISBN 978-0-87440-572-9
#15-B

CAST OF CHARACTERS
(In order of appearance)

Written for a Flexible Cast of Fifteen*
Approximately 5F, 4M, plus Extras

GLADYS, *the Pompington maid*
HENRY POMPINGTON, *a wealthy businessman*
MARIGOLD POMPINGTON, *his younger daughter*
PETUNIA POMPINGTON, *his older daughter*
ROVER, *Petunia's faithful dog*
REX HOLMES, *a wayfaring stranger*
VICTOR STRONGHEART, *Petunia's suitor*

CHARACTERS AROUND THE PLAY
(In Disorder of Appearance)

PIANO PLAYER (M or F)
DIRECTOR OF THE PLAY (M or F)
SCRUBWOMAN
STAGE MANAGER (M or F)
MAN BEHIND LADY IN HAT
LADY IN HAT
USHER (M or F)
PROMPTER OF THE PLAY (M or F)

* For greater possibilities of hilarity and fun, the play may be done with a cast of all women (including the male roles).

3

SYNOPSIS OF SCENES

SCENE 1—Drawing room of the Pompington home, early evening.

SCENE 2—Out in the snow, a few hours later.

SCENE 3—The drawing room, just before midnight.

The Scheme of the Driftless Shifter

SCENE ONE

(*As house lights go down, voices and general commotion can be heard backstage. There is then a sudden silence. When the audience has begun wondering what the delay might be, the* PIANO PLAYER *bursts noisily through door at rear of auditorium, races down center aisle, carrying a large stack of music. Obviously breathless, he tries to appear calm and collected as he nods briefly at the audience, settles himself at the piano, begins rummaging frantically through his music.*

Selecting a book, he props it on the rack, riffles through it, swiftly begins to play. Discovering at once that it is the wrong piece of music, he stops after the first few chords, casting a frightened, apologetic glance at the audience. Again he rummages through the stack of music, tries another piece from another book, discovers that it, too, is wrong. He stops again, rummages again, this time flinging one sheet of music after another over his shoulder. He tries another piece, which is not only the wrong one, but totally inappropriate. He continues it just the same, until the DIRECTOR *dashes wildly onstage from Left, hands him the correct book of music, swiftly exits.*

With a sigh of relief, PIANO PLAYER *begins playing, but manages only a few bars before he is interrupted by a* SCRUB-WOMAN, *carrying mop and bucket, who enters through auditorium door, Left, approaches piano.*)

SCRUBWOMAN. Okay, Buster, go do your practicing some place else. Rehearsal was supposed to be over at six.

PIANO PLAYER. This isn't the rehearsal. This is the *play!* We're just beginning!

SCRUBWOMAN. Listen, Mac, they told me six o'clock, that's all I know. Now scram. I've got work to do.

PIANO PLAYER. (*As* SCRUBWOMAN *begins mopping under piano*) But it's opening night! Don't you see the audience?

SCRUBWOMAN. They won't bother me. Lift your feet up a minute, will you? (PIANO PLAYER *obediently does so, as* SCRUBWOMAN *continues mopping*)

PIANO PLAYER. Look, it's a very short play. Couldn't you just take a seat somewhere and wait till it's over?

SCRUBWOMAN. (*Staring out into audience*) Well, the place *is* kinda cluttered up, I'll say that. You people sure have a lot of relatives. I hope they don't drop gum wrappers and stuff under the seats.

PIANO PLAYER. They're a very distinguished audience, I assure you. And they're all waiting for the play to begin. Say—wouldn't you like to see it yourself?

SCRUBWOMAN. I don't know. Is it any good?

PIANO PLAYER. Of *course* it's good! We've been rehearsing for weeks.

SCRUBWOMAN. Don't I know it! This place has been a mess every single night. I'll be glad when it's over.

PIANO PLAYER. It never will be, if you don't get out of here and let us get started.

SCRUBWOMAN. You've got a point there, honey. Well, okay. I'll wait. But make it snappy, will you? My feet are killing me and I want to get home early.

(SCRUBWOMAN *takes her time leaving, stomping slowly and heavily up center aisle.* PIANO PLAYER, *not wanting to start overture while* SCRUBWOMAN *is still in view, improvises music appropriate to her lumbering walk as* SCRUBWOMAN *heads for back of auditorium. Suddenly there is a loud crash backstage. It is the kind of crash in which, just when it seems to be all over, various smaller*

*crashes occur, one by one, as various other items drop to
the floor.* PIANO PLAYER, *looking startled, immediately
stops playing*)

STAGE MANAGER'S VOICE. (*From behind curtain, Stage
Left*) Watch it, you guys! Harry, didn't I tell you to get a good
grip on that thing? And look out for that vase. You're about
to—

(*There is another crash, this time clearly the sound of china
shattering*)

PIANO PLAYER. (*Leaping to his feet, shouting into the
curtain*) Hey, keep it quiet back there! The audience is here!
STAGE MANAGER. (*Poking his head out from behind
curtain, Left*) Yeah? Already? Hey, Harry, did you hear that?
They're here! Better get that stuff picked up.

(*Suddenly* VICTOR STRONGHEART *sticks his head in from
behind curtain, Stage Right*)

VICTOR. (*Excitedly*) Is it a good house? Have you counted?
STAGE MANAGER. Well, they're still coming in, but quite a
few rows are filled up.
VICTOR. How many?
STAGE MANAGER. Let's see now. One—two—three—
four—
VICTOR. Are there any Hollywood talent scouts, do you
think? I see a very important looking lady over there in the
fourth row.
STAGE MANAGER. Where?
VICTOR. There. (*Pointing*) The one in the black dress, with
the fur stole. Don't you think she looks important?
STAGE MANAGER. (*Spotting her, suddenly looking proud*)
Sure she does. That's my mother! Hi, Mom!

(*He waves cheerfully, as* VICTOR *looks disappointed.*
PETUNIA *sticks her head out through center of curtain*)

PETUNIA. (*All aflutter*) Did I hear somebody mention Hollywood talent scouts? Where? Where?

VICTOR. It's nobody. Just Charlie's mother.

STAGE MANAGER. And look—she's brought the whole family. There's my Aunt Mary, and Cousin Sue, and my little brother, Freddie—hi, Freddie!—and—

(*Suddenly* STAGE MANAGER *is yanked backward, Offstage Left, as* DIRECTOR *enters, looking flustered*)

DIRECTOR. (*Wildly waving his hands at* PETUNIA *and* VICTOR) Back, back! Nobody's supposed to see you yet! Not until the curtain!

STAGE MANAGER'S VOICE. Curtain? Is it time for the curtain? Already? Hey, did you hear that, Harry? Curtain!

(*At once curtain begins jerking open, to reveal clearly that onstage no one is ready.* GLADYS *is fixing hem of* MARIGOLD'S *dress;* POMPINGTON *and* HOLMES, *coatless and hatless, are seated at the table, playing gin rummy;* ROVER, *dog head in hand, is standing by, kibitzing. A couple of stagehands are just carrying in the fireplace. The* PIANO PLAYER *begins the overture just the same. Suddenly all onstage become aware of the situation. For one frozen moment they stare out at the audience, motionless. Then all scatter wildly to both sides of the stage. In a panic, the stagehands carry the fireplace out again. Noting the empty stage,* PIANO PLAYER *stops playing*)

DIRECTOR. (*Calling to* STAGE MANAGER) Stop, stop, you ninny! We're not ready!

STAGE MANAGER'S VOICE. But I thought you said—

DIRECTOR. I said stop!

STAGE MANAGER'S VOICE. I did stop. That's as far as it goes.

DIRECTOR. (*In despair*) I mean close it, close it! And tell Harry to get the stage ready. Bring back the fireplace. Tell him not to forget the fireplace! (*Turning pleasantly to audience, trying to make the best of a bad situation as curtain jerks shut once more*) I'm terribly sorry, ladies and gentlemen. These things do happen, but—ha ha!—that's show biz, as they say. If you'll just be patient, I'm sure our capable stage crew will have our stage ready in a minute or two, and the play will begin. So if you'll just settle back, relax, and—

> (*Suddenly a* MAN *in the audience, seated in aisle seat toward front, leaps to his feet*)

MAN BEHIND LADY IN HAT. (*Loudly*) If I've asked you once, I've asked you a dozen times! Will you *please* take off that idiotic hat? I can't see a thing!

LADY IN HAT. (*Rising, looking outraged*) This hat, sir, was made for me by Pierre Chapeau himself. It is an *original* Chapeau, and I have no intention whatever of removing it. I would suggest that *you* remove your *person* to another part of this auditorium.

MAN. Why should *I* move? I paid for this seat! Now you just take that silly contraption off your head, or I'll call the usher!

DIRECTOR. (*Nervously, not knowing what to do*) There are plenty of other seats, sir. Perhaps—

MAN. (*Furiously*) I want *this* seat! And I don't want to sit behind a blooming flower garden!

DIRECTOR. Perhaps, Madam, you could take it off now—and then you could put it on again—um—during intermission, when everyone can see it and admire it. Perhaps—

LADY. According to my program, there *is* no intermission. I will wear the hat *now!*

MAN. Usher! Usher!

LADY. (*As* USHER *rushes down aisle*) I am glad you are being sensible, sir. I was just going to call him myself. (*As* USHER *arrives*) Usher, will you kindly have this person removed? He is bothering me.

USHER. Sorry, lady. There's one in every audience. Come along, wise guy, and make it snappy. We don't want no troublemakers.

MAN. Hey, I'm no troublemaker! I just came to see the show, that's all. And I don't mean a flower show! Look at that thing, will you? It must be ten feet tall! And in full bloom!

USHER. (*Seizing* MAN's *arm*) Let's go, buddy.

MAN. But I want to see the show! I paid my money!

USHER. Out!

MAN. Okay. But the flower garden comes with me. Outside where it belongs!

(MAN *suddenly snatches hat from* LADY's *head, dashes up aisle with it, with* USHER *in hot pursuit.* LADY *cries out "My hat! My hat! Oh, my lovely Chapeau!" and runs after the two of them.* PIANO PLAYER, *knowing a good chase scene when he sees one, immediately plays chase music. Exit* MAN, USHER, LADY *at back of auditorium*)

DIRECTOR. (*To* PIANO PLAYER) Stop that noise, you nincompoop! That's not part of the play! (PIANO PLAYER *stops immediately, looking embarrassed*) Now then, ladies and gentlemen. I believe we are ready to begin. May I have the overture, please?

PIANO PLAYER. Now?

DIRECTOR. Yes, now.

PIANO PLAYER. Are you sure?

DIRECTOR. I'm sure! The overture, *please!*

(DIRECTOR *exits Left, overture begins, curtain opens to reveal drawing room set. This time, all is ready.* GLADYS *is onstage alone, whisking about with a feather duster. Overture continues as she struggles to make her first line heard. She says it several times*)

GLADYS. I wonder what can be keeping the mahster. I wonder what can be keeping the mahster. I wonder—what can be—KEEPING THE MAHSTER! (*Frustrated, she moves Downstage, bends over and swats* PIANO PLAYER *with her feather duster. He stops playing*) Such a cold night it is. I do hope he will be home soon. Ah, there he is now! I hear a knock at the door. (*There is no knock*) I—I—hear a knock at the door. (*Loud knock is suddenly heard*) It must be the mahster. I shall light the fire. (*She picks up a box of matches from the table, advances toward fireplace, striking a match as she goes. Light in fireplace blinks on before she reaches it. She bends to light the fire just the same*) There. All is in readiness. And I do believe I hear his knock again. (*There is no knock.* GLADYS *shrugs*) It is him.

PROMPTER. (*From Offstage Left, loudly*) He!

GLADYS. What?

PROMPTER. Not what—*who*.

GLADYS. Who?

PROMPTER. He!

GLADYS. (*Looking puzzled*) Oh. Well, I thought it was him all along. Yes, it is the mahster! At la-a-ast! I mean—at lahst! I shall open the door. (*Moves Left for routine that will happen throughout the play. Sound of door opening, sound of howling wind, snowflakes thrown in, sound of door closing*) Oh, what a cold night it is, sir. How heavily it is snowing!

POMPINGTON. (*Entering*) Yes, and my poor daughter, Petunia, is out driving in a sleigh with that dreadful cad, Victor Strongheart. I tried to stop her, but she is a headstrong girl, and left the house without my permission. Help me with my things, Gladys.

GLADYS. Yes, sir.

(POMPINGTON, *obviously a young man dressed up as an old man, removes his scarf and hat, hands both to* GLADYS. *Unfortunately, his white wig has come off along with the hat.* GLADYS, *looking horrified, quickly passes wig back to* POMPINGTON. *Trying to make nothing of it, he quickly shakes out the wig, sending clouds of cornstarch into the air, claps it back on his head. He then briefly warms his hands at the fireplace, takes his newspaper from the table, sits down to read*)

POMPINGTON. I am not late for dinner. I hope I was detained.

GLADYS. Beg Pardon, sir?

POMPINGTON. I am not late for dinner—

PROMPTER. I am not late for dinner *I hope*. I was detained.

POMPINGTON. Oh. Yes. Well—in any case, I am here.

GLADYS. Yes, sir. Dinner awaits, sir. Do you expect your lovely daughter, Petunia? And her handsome suitor, Mr. Victor Strongheart?

POMPINGTON. My lovely daughter, Petunia, yes. But not that penniless upstart who has stolen her heart. Never!

GLADYS. But why, sir? He is so handsome, sir.

POMPINGTON. Handsome, yes—but a worthless ne'er-do-well just the same. My daughter will not see him again.

(MARIGOLD, *carrying a doll, skips brightly in from Right, as* PIANO PLAYER *plays delicate "little girl" music*)

MARIGOLD. Why not, Father? Why will she not see him again? *I* think he's cute. And Petunia says she loves him.

POMPINGTON. She knows not whereof she speaks, my child. Her head has merely been turned by his good looks, his charm, his wit, his brilliance, his dashing manner. Nothing more.

MARIGOLD. What more is there, Father?

POMPINGTON. Ah, my child, how little you know of the cruel world. The young man has no background, no breeding, no family, no—

MARIGOLD. Money?

POMPINGTON. I would not wish to put it so crudely, my child. But facts must be faced. The young man is quite penniless.

MARIGOLD. But Petunia says she doesn't care. She is quite willing to live in a humble, rose-covered cottage, if only she and Victor can be together. Isn't that romantic?

POMPINGTON. Romantic—bah! Just as the roses on that humble cottage would soon food and drape—er—drade and foop—er—just as the roses would soon—

PROMPTER. Droop and fade!

POMPINGTON. Oh. Yes. Thank you. Just as the roses would soon droop and fade, so would our lovely Petunia. She would grow old before her time, working her delicate fingers to the bone, starving, suffering—and all for the love of a worthless vagabond. Here today, gone tomorrow—the very thought of his carefree life brings the scurl of corn—

MARIGOLD. Scurl of corn?

POMPINGTON. Corn of scurl—

PROMPTER. Curl of scorn! Brings the—

POMPINGTON. Oh, yes. Brings the curl of scorn to my lips. I will not have the scoundrel in my home. And that is final.

GLADYS. Then he will not be staying for dinner, sir?

POMPINGTON. He will not. Just go and answer the door.

GLADYS. The door, sir?

POMPINGTON. (*Listening for a knock, hearing none*) Yes, Gladys. I hear someone knocking now. (*Sudden knocking at door*) It must be my lovely daughter, Petunia. Go and let her in at once. Poor child, she must be frozen.

(GLADYS *answers door, Left.* PETUNIA *enters, all aglow, in a shower of snowflakes. She is followed by her faithful dog,* ROVER, *who licks* POMPINGTON'S *hand, then frolics about the room, obviously unable to see where he is going, bumps into furniture, knocks over a lamp. Helpfully, he rises to two feet and stands it up again. Then, on all fours again, he heads toward apron, nearly falls into the pit*)

POMPINGTON. (*Realizing his problem*) Sit, Rover, sit!

ROVER. Where? I can't see a darn thing in here!

POMPINGTON. (*Grasping him by the collar, leading him to fireplace*) Here, Rover, right by the fire. That's a good dog. (*Turning to* PETUNIA, *as* ROVER *settles himself, and* MARIGOLD *goes to sit beside him*) Ah, Petunia, here you are at last! I have been worrying about you.

(GLADYS *takes* PETUNIA'S *things, exits Right*)

PETUNIA. You need not have troubled yourself, Father, for I have had a glorious afternoon. My handsome suitor, Mr. Victor Strongheart, has proposed to me!

POMPINGTON. No!

PETUNIA. Yes! I said yes, Father! Mr. Strongheart will be coming here soon to ask formally for my hand.

POMPINGTON. He may not have it!

PETUNIA. But why, Father? He is such a splendid man. And he loves me. Will you not speak with him, Father?

POMPINGTON. Never! He is nothing but a drifter, like his father before him.

PETUNIA. You knew his father?

POMPINGTON. I knew him, daughter, years ago when his son was no more than a tiny baby. He was a very poor man, and one day the worthless rat left home, and was never seen again. He deserted his wife and child!

PETUNIA. Oh, Father, it was not like that at all. Victor has told me all about his father. The poor man wanted everything for his wife and child, but times were hard, and he could find no employment. And so—

POMPINGTON. And so he abandoned his poor sick wife and helpless infant!

PETUNIA. Abandoned! Oh no, Father. He had every intention of raising his son in the style to which—the style to which he would have liked to have—to—to have—the style to which he would have liked to have had him—

POMPINGTON. What?

PETUNIA. (*Relieved to be through with the line*) Become accustomed.

POMPINGTON. I see.

PETUNIA. And so he went away to seek his fortune in the California gold fields. His luck was not great at first, but soon he was able to send money home regularly. And then—

POMPINGTON. Yes?

PETUNIA. A terrible thing befell him. (*Ominous Chord*) He was wrongly accused of a crime he did not commit.

POMPINGTON. No!

PETUNIA. Yes! He was sent to prison, poor man, and there he languished for many years, awaiting pardon. And then, at the very moment of his release—

POMPINGTON. He was released?

PETUNIA. Yes, Father. And fully pardoned by the governor. There is now no blot upon the Strongheart name.

POMPINGTON. But why did he not come home, the bounder?

PETUNIA. Alas, Father, we do not know. For all those years he wrote faithfully to his wife and child, one letter each week. But when at last he was free, the letters suddenly stopped. (*Ominous Chord*) No one knew whether he was alive or dead, and dear, brave Victor has spent these many years searching for his lost father. And that is why he has not yet made his own fortune.

POMPINGTON. A sad story, daughter. But facts are facts. The young man is not only penniless, but the son of an ex-convict as well. And no daughter of—

PETUNIA. But Father—

POMPINGTON. No daughter of a convict will ever marry the son of a Pompington—I mean—no son of a Pompington—I mean—no daughter—I mean—

PETUNIA. (*Hastily saving the situation*) But I love him, Father!

MARIGOLD. (*Also helpful*) And he loves you.

PETUNIA. And—and—I love him.

MARIGOLD. And he—

POMPINGTON. Never mind! The likes of your penniless young man will never darken my doorstep.

PETUNIA. But he is not penniless, Father. Not any longer. Now that his poor mother, Anemia, has died of grief, he has given up the search and gone to work in the bank. Even now he is awaiting a promotion. I am sure he will soon be able to support me in the manner to which I am accustomed. Oh Father, do let him in.

POMPINGTON. What?

PETUNIA. I hear him knocking now. (*There is no knock.*) I hear him KNOCKING NOW! I— (*There is the sound of a doorbell*) —hear him knocking now. Please, dear Father, do not turn him away.

POMPINGTON. My word is final! (*Rushes to door, Left, receives huge handful of snowflakes in his face*) Go—and never darken my— (*Another handful of snow is thrown*) and never darken my— (*Still another handful comes his way, as he sputters*) Will you stop that?

STAGE MANAGER. (*Peering interestedly around curtain*)

But gee, I've got a whole basketful of this stuff. This is *fun!* *(Coming onstage, just enough to be clearly seen, turning to audience, waving)* Hi, Mom!

PROMPTER. *(As* STAGE MANAGER *moves back)* And never darken my—

POMPINGTON. —Door again! *(Door slams)* There. *(He jumps, as a final, unexpected handful of snow is thrown)* He is gone. Never to return. Forget him, daughter.

PETUNIA. No, Father, I will not forget him. I defy you!

POMPINGTON. You defy me?

PETUNIA. I defy you.

POMPINGTON. You— *(Frantically, to* PROMPTER*)* what comes next?

PROMPTER. I defy you.

POMPINGTON. I defy you?

PETUNIA. *(Flustered)* No. *I* defy *you.*

GLADYS. *(Entering hastily from Right, trying to help)* Dinner is served?

PROMPTER. Dinner is *not* served. That comes later. Go answer the door.

GLADYS. *(Confused, but still helpful)* I shall answer the door.

(Sound of knocking is suddenly heard)

POMPINGTON. *(Remembering his line)* Who can be ringing my doorbell at this hour?

*(*GLADYS *moves to open door, Left.* REX HOLMES *mistakenly enters Right, slinking furtively, as* PIANO PLAYER *plays villain entrance music,* GLADYS *receives usual handful of snow)*

GLADYS. *(Speaking toward Left anyhow)* Come right in, sir. Whom shall I say is calling?

HOLMES. *(Realizing his mistake, shouting across to her)* It is I, Rex Holmes, a wayfaring stranger.

GLADYS. *(Whirling)* Oh. Come right in, sir. Whom shall I say is—

POMPINGTON. (*Though* HOLMES *is standing right beside him, determined to say the right line*) Who is it, Gladys?

GLADYS. It is a Mr. Holmes, sir. Shall I—um—shall I show him in?

POMPINGTON. Yes, do. (*Aside, to audience*) I wonder why the dog is growling.

PROMPTER. (*As* ROVER *remains silent*) Rover!

ROVER. (*Startled*) What?

PROMPTER. Grrrrr!

ROVER. Oh. Grrrrr!

POMPINGTON. I wonder why the dog is growling. Is there something to fear from this wayfaring stranger? (*To* HOLMES) Ah, good evening, sir. How kind of you to drop in. May I introduce my lovely daughters? This is my lovely daughter Petunia (PETUNIA *curtseys*) and this is my lovely daughter Marigold. (MARIGOLD *does the same, but hides behind* PETUNIA)

HOLMES. I am pleased to meet you, lovely daughters. (*Rubbing his hands together*) More pleased than you think!

MARIGOLD. Why?

HOLMES. You shall see, little one, you shall see.

POMPINGTON. What business brings you out on such a night, Mr. Holmes? I note your interest in my lovely daughters. Perhaps you are an encyclopedia salesman?

HOLMES. I am selling nothing, sir. But I wish to do important business with you. It is a matter of high finance.

POMPINGTON. High finance, eh? (*He leans casually on the mantelpiece, discovers its flimsiness, immediately straightens*) Then I take it you are a businessman?

HOLMES. In a manner of speaking, yes.

GLADYS. Will he be staying for dinner, sir? Shall I set another place?

POMPINGTON. By all means. We must make our guest welcome. Set the table for four, Gladys.

GLADYS. Yes, sir. (*Exits Right*)

HOLMES. I shall not be staying.

POMPINGTON. But why not? I'm sure we have more than enough for four.

HOLMES. Then it will be a very hearty meal, sir. For—heh,

heh!—there will be only two of you at the dinner table this night.

GLADYS. (*Sticking her head in, Right*) Two, did he say, sir?

POMPINGTON. Our guest will not be staying for dinner, Gladys. You may bring us some tea instead. Tea for two.

GLADYS. Yes, sir. Tea for two.

(PIANO PLAYER *suddenly breaks into rendition of "Tea for Two." * DIRECTOR *dashes onstage at once, angrily draws finger across his throat.* PIANO PLAYER *stops*)

POMPINGTON. I do not understand you, sir. My lovely daughters and I are a family of three. Why do you say there will only be two for dinner?

HOLMES. Because—heh, heh!—I intend to kidnap one of your lovely daughters!

POMPINGTON. (*Aghast*) You do not mean it!

HOLMES. I do mean it!

POMPINGTON. (*Forgetting his next line*) You—do not mean it!

HOLMES. I do mean it!

POMPINGTON. You do not—you—um—you do not—

GLADYS. (*Poking her head in from Right, again helpful*) Dinner is served?

PROMPTER. Dinner is *not* served!

GLADYS. Then—shall I answer the door? (*Starts toward Left*)

PROMPTER. No. There is no one at the door.

(GLADYS *withdraws*)

POMPINGTON. (*Loudly, mistaking this for his line*) There is no one at the door.

HOLMES. (*Trying to get things back where they started*) I do mean it. I mean to kidnap one of your lovely daughters. I—I—

PROMPTER. I am a desperate man.

POMPINGTON. (*Thinking the line is his*) I am a desperate man.

PROMPTER. No, no, not you—*him. He* is a desperate man!

POMPINGTON. He is a desperate—

HOLMES. (*Taking hold*) I am a desperate man. I have fallen on hard times, and I am penniless. I have a fine son, sir, and I would not wish him to see me so. And so I am driven to this evil deed.

POMPINGTON. You would not—

HOLMES. I would! I shall take this golden, tiny-haired tot—this—this—tiny, golden-haired tot, your lovely daugher—uh—What's-er-name—and then I shall demand ransom.

(*During this speech,* MARIGOLD *claps her hands to her head, realizing that she has forgotten her golden wig, dashes Left, where* STAGE MANAGER'S *hand comes out with wig.* MARIGOLD *hastily puts it on, somewhat lopsided, returns demurely to her place*)

POMPINGTON. How—how much? I have a considerable sum in my vault, and—

HOLMES. Five million dollars! (*Ominous Chord*)

POMPINGTON. Oh!

HOLMES. Payable by midnight tonight! If I do not receive the money promptly, then you will never see this innocent child again!

POMPINGTON. Midnight! (*Ominous Chord*)

HOLMES. Midnight. You will have your lovely daughter back, sir, when the money has been paid. And not a moment before! Come, lovely daughter.

(HOLMES *starts dragging* MARIGOLD *Off Right, as sound of door opening, wind howling, is heard, snow is thrown in from Left*)

MARIGOLD. (*Yanking* HOLMES *toward Left*) This way, you dummy!

(*Both exit Left amid a second dose of snow. Door slams*)

PETUNIA. Oh Father, what shall we do? It is already eight o'clock. Hark! Do you not hear the clock striking? (*They listen, as no clock strikes*) Do you not HEAR THE CLOCK STRIKING? (*Suddenly a clock begins slowly striking. It strikes five times*) Yes, Father, it is already eight o'clock. Oh, what is to become of us?

POMPINGTON. (*In despair*) I do not know, daughter. There is no one to help us.

PETUNIA. There is, Father, there is! My strongheart, Victor Sweetheart—I mean—my sweetheart, Victor Strongheart. He can do anything.

POMPINGTON. Bah! He is nothing but a driftless shifter!

PROMPTER. A shiftless drifter!

PETUNIA. No, Father, he is not a— (*Not daring to say the phrase*) he is a brave and noble person. I know he can find little Marigold for us, and bring that blackhearted villain to justice. I shall go now, Father, out into the snow, and I shall find Victor Strongheart! He will save us!

POMPINGTON. But the storm, daughter—

PETUNIA. No matter, Father. Remember—it is always darkest before the dawn!

POMPINGTON. Yes!

PETUNIA. A bird in the hand is worth two in the bush!

POMPINGTON. Yes!

PETUNIA. A stitch in time saves nine!

POMPINGTON. Yes, yes!

PETUNIA. A penny saved is a penny earned!

POMPINGTON. Yes! Oh, daughter, you are so wise! I know you will succeed! Go, now, and Godspeed! And I shall put a candle in every window!

(POMPINGTON *dramatically exits Right, as* PETUNIA *puts on her shawl and starts toward door, Left*)

PETUNIA. Come, Rover. Come, my faithful dog. (*As* ROVER *starts blindly in the opposite direction*) We will go bravely out into the storm, we will find Victor, we will—Rover!

ROVER. (*Raising his dog head, looking frantically about, discovering his mistake*) Oh. Sorry!

(*He replaces the head and follows* PETUNIA. *The two exit*

Left amid huge handfuls of snow, sound of wind. When the stage is deserted, GLADYS *enters Right, crosses to center, looks blankly about)*

GLADYS. (*Uncertainly*) Dinner is served?

CURTAIN

SCENE TWO

To be played before the curtain
PETUNIA *enters Right, in a shower of snow, followed by* ROVER

PETUNIA. Oh, where can he be? Victor! Victor! Where are you? Oh, it is so cold! I may freeze to death. Yes, I believe I will die, out here in the snow! Victor! Victor! (*She staggers across stage to Center, sinks wearily to floor. Handfuls of snow are continuously dumped on her by very obvious hand coming through center of curtain.* ROVER *licks her face.* PIANO PLAYER *plays suitable dying music*) It is no use, my faithful dog. I cannot go on. This is the end. All is over.

(*Raising her arms dramatically,* PETUNIA *is about to launch into her next line, but gets no farther than "I—" when suddenly the* SCRUBWOMAN *calls out from halfway down center aisle, begins lumbering heavily toward stage*)

SCRUBWOMAN. (*Loudly*) All over, did you say? Are you through?
PETUNIA. (*In a stage whisper*) Of course not! This is my big scene!
SCRUBWOMAN. But you said it was the end!
PETUNIA. Well, it isn't. I mean, it's not the end of the play. Now get out of here. I'm supposed to be dying.
SCRUBWOMAN. (*Arriving at the apron*) Then it must be the end. What more could you do? (*Reaching up onstage for handful of snow*) Hey, what's all this white stuff doing all over my nice clean floor? Boy, you show people really make a mess!

PETUNIA. Will you please go—and let me die in peace?

SCRUBWOMAN. Well, okay. But don't be too long about it, will you, honey? I wanna get home early. My feet are killing me.

(SCRUBWOMAN *stomps back up aisle, as* PIANO PLAYER *plays exit music,* PETUNIA *tries to be heard above it*)

PETUNIA. I cannot go on. This is the end. All is over. (*Shouting toward* PIANO PLAYER) I said—ALL IS OVER! (PIANO PLAYER *immediately switches back to dying music*) But hark! Do I not hear footsteps? Oh Rover, can it be him?

PROMPTER. He! Can it be *he!*

PETUNIA. (*Exasperated*) Okay, *okay!* Gee—everybody's spoiling my scene! Can it be *he?*

VICTOR. (*Bounding in from Left, to rousing hero music*) Yes, my sweetheart, it is me—it is I! It is I, Victor Strongheart. I have come to save you. (*Clearly enjoying his moment of glory,* VICTOR *makes the most of his opening speech, uttering his lines as though he were playing Hamlet. Completely ignoring* PETUNIA, *he bounds dramatically from one side of the stage to the other*) You shall not die, my darling, no! You are the love of my life, my sweetest, you— (*As he dashes about more and more swiftly,* PIANO PLAYER *is inspired to switch from Dying Music to Chase Music,* VICTOR, *clearly annoyed that the music is drowning out his voice, briefly stops Center Stage, mutters "Will you shut up?", then continues his lines as* PIANO PLAYER *abruptly stops playing*) You are the love of my life, my sweetest, you are the stars and the moon, you are everything to me. You shall not die, while I have my strength. For the strength of a Strongheart is strong. No, you shall not die. We will be together forever, my lovely one, and—

PETUNIA. (*Furiously, as* VICTOR *keeps stumbling past her*) VICTOR!

VICTOR. Oh. There you are, my pet. (*Taking one last, lingering moment to display his handsome self to audience,* VICTOR *finally kneels beside* PETUNIA, *continues thundering his lines out toward audience*) Come, lovely one. My sleigh awaits. I shall take you home to your devoted father and your loving sister.

PETUNIA. My dear little sister, alas, is not at home. She has been abducted by a wicked villain.

VICTOR. No!

PETUNIA. Yes! And he is demanding five million dollars ransom. My father is a rich man, but a demand like this would bring him down to his last million. He would be a broken man. Oh, Victor, what shall we do? Where can we get five million dollars?

VICTOR. (*Rising*) We shall not need it, my love. Remember—the strength of a Strongheart is stronger than the strength of the strengest—the strength—the strength—

PETUNIA. What?

VICTOR. (*Starting over*) We shall not need it, my love. Remember—the strength—

PETUNIA. (*Saving him*) Yes, Victor, I remember. And I know that you, Victor Strongheart—

VICTOR. Yes, yes, that's it exactly. I, Victor Strongheart, will find your dear sister, and I will bring her wicked captor to justice. But first, my sweet, I will take you home to your dear father. Come. Let us go.

(*Flurries of snow from here, there and everywhere as the two exit Left.* ROVER, *after considerable confusion, stumbles Off Right*)

BLACKOUT

SCENE THREE

Curtain opens to reveal PETUNIA, *collapsed and shivering on chair, Stage Right.* POMPINGTON *is kneeling beside her, rubbing her hands.* ROVER, *whose Scene Two exit was in the wrong direction, races in, Upright, from Left, settles himself at* PETUNIA's *feet*

POMPINGTON. Poor child—you are quite frozen! You must have a nice hot cup of tea. I shall ring for Gladys at once. (*He rises, yanks sharply on the bell pull. It comes immediately off the wall, falls in a crumpled heap to the floor. He stares at it for a moment, perplexed, then calls loudly Offstage Right*) GLADYS!

GLADYS. (*Entering Right*) You rang, sir?

POMPINGTON. Yes, Gladys. My lovely daughter Petunia has been out in the storm and is chilled to the bone. Please go at once and fetch her a nice hot cup of tea.

GLADYS. Yes, sir. And will you be wanting some too, sir?

POMPINGTON. Yes, thank you, Gladys.

GLADYS. Then it will be—tea for two?

(*To* POMPINGTON's *annoyance,* PIANO PLAYER *immediately launches into "Tea for Two"*)

POMPINGTON. (*Striding angrily Downstage toward* PIANO PLAYER) Never mind, Gladys. (*Thundering at* PIANO PLAYER) I WILL HAVE *COFFEE* INSTEAD! (PIANO PLAYER *slips easily into rendition of "You're the Cream in My Coffee"*) *BLACK!* (PIANO PLAYER *stops*)

GLADYS. Yes, sir. (*Exits Right as loud knocking is heard*)

POMPINGTON. Hark! The village clock is striking. Do you not hear it?

PETUNIA. I hear it! Oh Father, can it be midnight already? (*Knocking is heard again*) Can it be—MIDNIGHT already? (*Clock suddenly strikes slowly 5 times*) Yes, Father, I believe the hour has come. (*All in a rush, clock strikes 7 more times, then adds 1 more, to make the total 13*) Oh, what can be keeping Victor?

POMPINGTON. (*Confused*) Hark! The village clock—

PETUNIA. (*Trying to help*) The clock has already struck, Father. Oh, what can be keeping Victor?

POMPINGTON. Hark!

PETUNIA. I *am* harking, Father. The clock has already—

PROMPTER. Sleighbells! Sleighbells!

POMPINGTON. Ah, yes! Hark, daughter, do you not hear the sound of—

PIANO PLAYER. (*Leaping to his feet in a panic, calling into the curtain*) The sleighbells! Quick, the sleighbells!
STAGE MANAGER'S VOICE. (*Loudly*) Hey, Harry, have you got the sleighbells? Harry?

(*There is a long silence. Suddenly* STAGE MANAGER *dashes onstage from Left, flings sleighbells to* PIANO PLAYER, *who frantically rings them*)

POMPINGTON. Do you not hear the sound of sleighbells?
PETUNIA. Yes, Father—but so far away! It may be hours before Victor can make his way through the storm.

(*There is an immediate knocking*)

POMPINGTON. Ah, there he is now. I do hope he has found my lovely daughter, Marigold. I shall open the door at once.

(*Before he does so,* MARIGOLD *skips merrily in from Left, amid shower of snow, sound of wind, delicate entrance music*)

MARIGOLD. I am home, dear Father, safe and sound! Petunia's intended, Victor Strongheart, has saved me from a terrible fate. I might have perished in the snow, had it not been for Victor Strongheart!
PETUNIA. I knew he could do it, Father, I knew! Come, dear sister, and warm yourself by the fire. Gladys has just gone out for some nice hot—
POMPINGTON. (*To* PIANO PLAYER) For some nice hot—COCOA!

(*Doorbell rings*)

PETUNIA. I hear—a knocking at the door, Father. It must be Victor. Let him in, Father, let him in.
POMPINGTON. I shall indeed, my daughter. The poor penniless young man must be rewarded for his noble deed. (*Rushes*

to open door, Left. Usual wind, snow, door slam as VICTOR *enters, bounding to Center stage, accompanied by hero music)* Come in, poor penniless young man. You will be handsomely rewarded.

VICTOR. *(Proudly)* I would not take money for my noble deed, sir.

POMPINGTON. But why? I am sure you are in great need.

VICTOR. No longer, sir. For just today, I have received a fine promotion. I am now the president of the bank. Besides that, I have received a large inheritance from my dear rich aunt in Schenectady. I am far from penniless, sir. I am, in fact, a very rich man.

PETUNIA. Oh, Father, just think! Victor can now support me in the style to which I am accustomed! I do hope this will influence your decision.

POMPINGTON. *(Thoughtfully, to audience)* It does make a difference.

VICTOR. There is something else you should know, sir. I am not only rich, I am brave as well. For singlehanded, I have captured the worthless bounder who abducted your lovely daughter, Marigold.

POMPINGTON. How did you do it?

VICTOR. It was nothing, sir, really nothing. All it took was a keen mind, a loving heart, a strong body, a dashing manner, a kindly disposition, a brilliant wit, and the courage of a lion. It was nothing any man of these qualifications could not have done.

POMPINGTON. And where is the worthless bounder now?

VICTOR. He is at your very door, sir, too weak and faint-hearted to attempt escape. Do you wish to speak with him before I turn him over to the proper authorities?

POMPINGTON. I do. He must be sternly admonished for his evil deed. Let him in at once.

VICTOR. Yes, sir. *(Dashing to door, Left, opening it to usual snow and wind)* Come in, worthless bounder. *(Once again* REX HOLMES *makes wrong entrance, slinking in from Right, to villain music. He stands with head hanging)* There he is, sir—

(*Whirling about to spot* HOLMES) There he is, sir, an evil and unrepentant cad.

HOLMES. But I do repent!

POMPINGTON. (*Approaching him*) You do?

HOLMES I do. I—I— (*Clearly he has forgotten his next line*)

POMPINGTON. You do?

HOLMES. I do. I—I—

POMPINGTON. You—

HOLMES. (*Remembering*) I could not go through with my wicked scheme. Even as this splendid young man found us wandering in the storm, we were on our way back to you. I could not do it.

POMPINGTON. But why not?

HOLMES. Because, sir, this innocent child, your lovely daughter, Zinnia—

POMPINGTON. Marigold!

HOLMES. —Your lovely daughter, Marigold, reminded me of my own long lost son, Victor.

VICTOR. You had a son called—Victor?

HOLMES. I did. But I have not seen him for many years. Nor have I seen his lovely mother, my wife, Anemia, who has since died.

VICTOR. Anemia, you say?

HOLMES. Yes. Anemia Strongheart. That was her name.

POMPINGTON. But your name is Holmes!

HOLMES. Alas, sir, that is but an assumed name. If I should ever find my long lost son, Victor, I would not wish him to know me as a desperate criminal.

VICTOR. But your real name is—Rex Strongheart?

HOLMES. It is.

VICTOR. Father!

HOLMES. Son! (*The two embrace*) Can you ever forgive me?

VICTOR. Of course, dear Father. I am not only rich and brave, I am also kind.

HOLMES. I knew it. You are like your dear mother, my son. Poor soul. How she must have suffered, wondering where her long lost husband might be. But I could not write.

VICTOR. Why, Father? Why did the letters suddenly stop?

HOLMES. Because, my dear son, I was ashamed. The stigma of my imprisonment followed me everywhere, and I could find no employment.

VICTOR. But you were fully pardoned by the governor, were you not?

HOLMES. I was. But it is a cruel, cruel world, my son, and despite my innocence, I was looked upon everywhere as nothing more than an ex-convict. And so, alas, I was never able to make the fortune I wanted so much for you and your mother. And that is why I was driven to the desperate measure of attempting to kidnap this lovely child.

VICTOR. But you could not do it, Father, could you? You could not do it because at heart you are kind and good and strong and fine and brave and noble. How like me you are, Father!

HOLMES. But alas, my son, I am a poor man.

VICTOR. No longer! I shall get you a position in the bank, Father, and in no time at all you will be nearly as rich as I.

PETUNIA. Oh, Father, did you ever see a young man so noble as Victor Strongheart? So strong, so brave, so—so—

MARIGOLD. Rich?

PETUNIA. So kind, so—

MARIGOLD. —Cute! Don't forget cute!

PETUNIA. So cute! Oh, Father, will you not change your decision?

POMPINGTON. Of course, my child. I could ask no finer husband for my lovely daughter.

PETUNIA. Then we can be married?

POMPINGTON. We shall make the plans at once, lovely daughter. But first, let us all have a festive dinner together. I shall ring for Gladys. I shall— (*He moves to where bell pull was, sees that it is on the floor, shouts as before*) GLADYS! (GLADYS *enters Right, carrying tray with cups and saucers*) Is dinner ready?

GLADYS. Dinner will be served in a moment, sir. And in the meantime, I have brought cocoa for little Marigold, I have brought coffee for you and Mr. Holmes. And for your lovely daughter Petunia, and her handsome suitor, Mr. Strongheart, I have brought—

POMPINGTON. Don't say it!

GLADYS. I have brought—tea for two!

(PIANO PLAYER *immediately strikes up "Tea for Two," continues playing as all line up for Curtain Call.* DIRECTOR, PROMPTER, STAGE MANAGER *enter from Right.* LADY IN HAT *and* MAN BEHIND LADY IN HAT, *now arm in arm, come up the aisle, Left, to join the others onstage.* USHER, *carrying flowers, comes up center aisle, hands flowers up to stage. There is confusion as both* PETUNIA *and* DIRECTOR *step forward to receive them, step back, then step forward again. While they are trying to decide which of them gets the flowers,* MARIGOLD *dashes forward and snatches them, bowing happily as* PETUNIA *and* DIRECTOR *look disappointed and angry.* SCRUBWOMAN *enters from Left, pushing her mop across the stage in front of the cast. Noticing the audience, she stops to bob a curtsey, then continues mopping, exits Right. All the while,* DIRECTOR *is very obviously nudging* STAGE MANAGER, *who is enjoying his moment onstage, is waving to his mother. Finally he gets the* DIRECTOR'S *message*)

STAGE MANAGER. (*Calling Offstage Right*) Okay, Harry! That's it!

(*Curtain closes, then unexpectedly opens once more, to reveal pandemonium. Stagehands are already removing fireplace.* PETUNIA *is grappling with* MARIGOLD *for possession of the flowers. Various actors are congratulating each other.* ROVER *has removed his head,* HOLMES *his moustache. All dash back into line once more, as, finally,*

THE CURTAIN FALLS

PRODUCTION NOTES

SETTING:
A drawing room. Stage Center is a fireplace, flimsily constructed, with light behind fabricated fire. To left are 2 chairs, to right 1 chair and a low table. An old-fashioned bell pull hangs on wall to Left of fireplace.

PROPS:
Mop
Bucket
Feather duster
Snow (torn-up paper, or bits of styrofoam)
Tray with cups and saucers
Newspaper
Stack of music
Doll
Flowers for Curtain Call
Coat and Hat rack

COSTUMES AND MAKE-UP:
POMPINGTON—Business suit and hat. Powdered white wig, lightly stuck to hat. Scarf.
PETUNIA—Long dress, girlishly sweet. Shawl. Fur hat.
MARIGOLD—Sweet little-girl dress. Golden wig.
VICTOR—Neat suit, bright colored and dashing. Jaunty cap. Scarf.
HOLMES—Dark, shabby coat, black hat, obviously fabricated moustache.
GLADYS—Maid uniform with cap and apron.
ROVER—Dog costume with collar, removable head or face mask that can be lifted.

PIANO PLAYER—Bright jacket, bow tie. (Pretty dress with corsage for female)

DIRECTOR—Neat "dressed-up" outfit, with large corsage for female, boutonniere for male.

STAGE MANAGER—Overalls or jeans, bright shirt.

LADY IN HAT—Fancy outfit, perhaps with stole or feather boa, enormous flower hat.

MAN BEHIND LADY—Neat suit.

USHER—Neat suit with boutonniere.

SCRUBWOMAN—Dowdy dress or skirt with uneven hem, long sagging cardigan, heavy work boots, scarf on head, a few large curlers.

SOUND EFFECTS:

All to be done by PIANO PLAYER,* in full view of audience. Three chimes, two for doorbell, one for clock striking. Sound of door opening and shutting can be done by opening and shutting piano bench. For sleighbells, set of hand bells. Sound of knocking, mallet on block of wood. Sound of wind should be on wind effects record. Baker's can supply such a record, number 1017.

SPECIAL EFFECTS:

Light in fireplace to be lighted from offstage.

If a follow-spot is available, it could be used to great comic effect, especially if it bobs uncertainly about and lands in all the wrong places. Suggested uses:

Scene One:

A spot might precede the PIANO PLAYER's entrance, landing on the piano, discovering him missing, then bobbing frantically about in search of him.

The spot might also follow entrances and exits of SCRUBWOMAN, MAN and LADY IN HAT. It could also spot MAN and LADY while they are having their argument in the audience.

* Except for sound of crashing backstage at beginning of play.

Scene Two:
As VICTOR strides back and forth saying his lines, the spot could dart in opposite directions, with VICTOR in frantic pursuit of it.

MUSIC:

For wrong opening music at beginning of play, suggest opening bars of well-known musicals (OKLAHOMA, FIDDLER ON THE ROOF, etc.)

Overture can be any old-time melodrama music.

PIANO PLAYER needs to know all of "Tea for Two," first phrase of "You're the Cream in My Coffee."

All other music (Chase, Dying, Villain, etc.) should be in old-time melodrama style.

MISCELLANEOUS:

PROMPTER, script in hand, should lean far enough out onstage while giving lines to be seen by audience.

MURDER AT THE GREY'S HOUND MANSION
Maxine Holmgren

Mystery, High School/ Community Theatre / 5f, 3m / *Simple Set*
This is a mysterious comedy (or a comical mystery) that will have everyone howling with laughter.

The eccentric owner of Grey's Hound Mansion has been murdered. The cast gathers at the gloomy mansion for the reading of the will. Lightning lights up the stage as thunder and barking dogs greet the wacky characters that arrive. Each one is a suspect, and each one suspects another. Mixed metaphors and alliterations will have the audience barking up the wrong tree until the mystery is solved.

Baker's Plays
7611 Sunset Blvd.
Los Angeles, CA 90046
Phone: 323-876-0579
Fax: 323-876-5482

BAKERSPLAYS.COM

STONE SOUP
Anne Glasner & Betty Hollinger

Musical, TYA/Children's Theatre / 9m, 7f, 2 either / Simple Set
2 hungry soldiers stumble on a town filled with disgruntled neighbors. Using their imaginations, the soldiers trick the townsfolk into donating seasonings for their legendary Stone Soup, which they have convinced the townsfolk is a delicacy beyond measure. They con the townfolk into giving them all the ingredients to make a real soup, and in doing so, the soldiers help the townsfolk learn how to get along with each other by working together to create something good.

Baker's Plays
7611 Sunset Blvd.
Los Angeles, CA 90046
Phone: 323-876-0579
Fax: 323-876-5482

BAKERSPLAYS.COM

THE ANGRY EAGLE FEATHER
Julie Tosh

Modern Fable / 6m., 4f. / Unit Set

From the author of Beauty of the Century and Pharaoh's Revenge comes a beautiful modem Native American fable with a universal message. Ruth MacAfferty has a problem. First of all, for a third grader she gets too much homework. She also has a disinterested older brother Jacob and a know-it-all older sister Sarah. But life as she knows it comes to a crashing halt when a golden eagle feather falls from the sky to land at her feet. Her first mistake is picking it up. Her second is telling anyone she has it. Because now Ruth is a criminal. She is breaking the law of the United States by possessing a protected religious symbol of Native American tribes everywhere. On top of that, the feather has started talking to her, and it isn't happy sitting in her backpack day after day. Jacob thinks she should see someone in government. Sarah thinks she should take it back to where she got it. But, when Ruth's teacher suggests she get help at the nearby reservation. Ruth and her angry eagle feather both find a spiritual home.

Baker's Plays
7611 Sunset Blvd.
Los Angeles, CA 90046
Phone: 323-876-0579
Fax: 323-876-5482

BAKERSPLAYS.COM